Cotswold
Landscape

Photographs by F.A.H. Bloemendal
Text by Alan Hollingsworth

LONDON
IAN ALLAN LTD

CONTENTS

Previous page:
A Cotswold idyll . . . the Gloucestershire
village of Lower Slaughter in the valley of
the Eye stream epitomises the ageless
appeal of sparkling limestone houses in
gentle wooded limestone hills.

Right:
Dusk on the Cotswold escarpment above
Broadway looking westwards into
Worcestershire. Bredon Hill and the
Malvern Hills are in the background.

First published 1991

ISBN 0 7110 1959 2

Published by Ian Allan Ltd, Shepperton,
Surrey; and printed in Italy by
Athesia Druck GmbH, Bozen

Introduction

People have been drawn to the Cotswolds since the beginning of human settlement in these islands and that attraction remains as strong at the end of the 20th century as it did in the Stone Age. My own love affair with them began long ago when at the age of 19 I learned to fly at a little airfield called Watchfield on the edge of the Cotswolds in the Vale of White Horse — and few people learn to read and appreciate the local countryside quicker than do anxious novice pilots. In what was then for me a totally new experience in a totally new countryside — I came from Lincolnshire — the gentle rounded curves of the hills, the snaking drystone walls and the sparkling streams, and above all the brilliant grey-gold limestone of the farmhouses on the hillsides and the villages in the valleys were to captivate my heart even more surely than did the more immediate charms of the dear old de Havilland Tiger Moth. The love affair continued when in later years I lived first near Burford, then just outside Cirencester, and later in the Chippenham area. It strengthened after a long association with Broadway and was finally consummated when I worked with Frederick Bloemendal on his first Cotswold book over 10 years ago.

Nowhere in England — or indeed few places elsewhere in Britain — are landscape and buildings quite so closely and so harmoniously linked as they are in the Cotswolds. In few areas is the underlying rock so malleable and so visually appealing. The granites of Devon and Cornwall produce grandeur in both scenery and buildings but are hard to work and therefore limited in their use for humbler human dwellings. The wide variety of sandstones suitable for building, like those of the Peak District and the Pennine ridge, have their own rugged appeal in rugged country but, especially when blackened by industrial effluvia, lack the harmony and homely warmth of the Cotswold limestone. Slate is the natural material for tiling brick houses but walls built of it need a coat of colour wash to bring them to life. The chalk country like the Sussex Downs or the Lincolnshire Wolds has delightful rolling hills like the Cotswolds but you can't build much with chalk. Thus apart from the ubiquitous flint, the heritage of attractive houses in those areas usually owes more to the local brickworks and timber yards than to the quarries. There are also other limestones but few of them as easily quarried or as easily worked as those of the Cotswolds.

This book looks primarily at the heritage of the Cotswolds in its landscape form — the rolling hills, the gentle valleys, the stone villages and the mellow townscapes as seen by the eye of one of Europe's most gifted landscape photographers.

Cotswold Stone

Most of the Cotswold stone we see above ground rejoices in the name of 'freestone' and opinions on the origin of that name vary. Some say that it is 'free' because neatly rectangular slabs suitable for the tight-jointed high quality building method we call 'ashlar' can be lifted straight out of the rock face. Others that because of its fine texture masons can cut it freely in any direction with a saw — and hence are 'freemasons' (as distinct from 'rough' masons who build from uncut rubble). Either way or both, the ease with which Cotswold stone can be cut, carved and sculpted and the way in which it hardens after exposure to the weather has made it highly sought after since men first built in stone. The unmistakable Cotswold style of building evolved in the Middle Ages from the sheer workability of the local stone and has been copied all along the belt where similar stone can be found from South Dorset to South Lincolnshire. So let us now look rather more closely at this Cotswold stone and at the Cotswold building style which shows it off so well.

Geologically, Cotswold stone is an oolitic limestone of the Jurassic period. For those whose minds usually close at this point, there is a helpful analogy on the history of the origins of Cotswolds limestone which I have long cherished. It comes from a book by the late H. J. Massingham who in 1947 instigated one of the early Cotswolds conservation societies, the Men of the Stones. In his book *Cotswold Country,* which appeared in about 1937, he says that the limestone of the Cotswold region is among what he calls 'Thursday's Stones'. If, he argues, it took six days to create the Earth and today is the seventh or Sabbath when we are enjoying the fruits of that Creation, then the Jurassic period when the Cotswold stone was made would have been Thursday — between c135 and c185 million years ago — geologically the day before yesterday. 'The day just before the humble were exalted and the little mammals stepped into the kingdom of the great saurians, the day that is called Jurassic.'

The oolitic type of limestone laid down during the Jurassic period which is most visible in the Cotswolds takes its name from the Greek 'oo' or egg and 'lith', stone, hence 'egg-stone' because it is made up of

Left:

Crickley Hill The Cotswold escarpment seen from the A417 near Barrow Wake just outside Gloucester. Churchdown Hill, a remnant of an earlier escarpment, is in the background. Crickley Hill itself is 900ft (295m) above sea-level and is surmounted by an Iron Age fort created by dragging up large blocks of limestone and covering them with earth. The cliffs below the escarpment are composed of a 40ft (10m) layer of limestone known as 'pea grit' composed of ovoid grains about the size of a pea similar to the smaller egg-shaped grains of the oolite. It is a crumbly rock not suitable for building and earlier in geological time than Cotswold stone. The cliffs are very rich in the fossils of primitive creatures like sea-urchins and provide a popular attraction for geologists. The wooded area above the cliff is known as 'The Scrubbs' and includes part of the Iron Age fort. It is owned by the National Trust and offers splendid views over the Severn Valley.

spherical grains like tiny eggs. (A better name is used by quarrymen who call it 'roestone' — like a fish roe. So Cotswold stone, you might say, is a caviar among building stones.) If we extend Massingham's analogy a little further, then if the Jurassic series of rocks were created during some cosmic Thursday, the oolite layers were laid down on that cosmic Thursday morning when the sun was shining. Whereas clays come from the nocturnal depths of dull muddy seas, sandstones from the twilight of clouded silt-laden seas, the limestones indicate clear sunlit shallow seas like those found nowadays around Bermuda or Australia's Great Barrier Reef. In such waters corals lie, reproduce and die and their skeletons saturate the water in calcium bicarbonate and the sea's constant movement causes tiny organic particles to become coated with concentric layers of calcium carbonate — hence our ooliths. And hence too, perhaps, that curious and unique quality of the Cotswold oolite to reflect the shifting tones of the day, lighting up like silver gilt in the sunlight and purpling down in the shadows.

Earlier on that same geological Thursday — and hence below the oolites in the stack of rocks that makes up the Jurassic 'series' or layers — were laid down the sandier 'lias' levels. Later in the day and above the oolites come various clays including, in the Cotswold area, the Oxford and the Kimmeridge clays.

What in mid-Jurassic times would have been part of a northern hemisphere's 'Great Barrier Reef' and basking under tropical sunshine runs diagonally across England in a great arc from Lyme Bay in Dorset to the mouth of the Tees. The oolitic limestone begins at Burton Bradstock on the Dorset coast, runs northeastwards as a narrow band never more than five miles wide and sometimes down to less than a mile to just north of Bath where it widens steadily to reach a maximum of about 30 miles along the axis of the A40 between Witney and Cleeve Hill above Cheltenham. It narrows again in the valley of the Cherwell south of Banbury to continue north as a narrow belt through Northamptonshire and Lincolnshire to the Humber where it peters out, recurring again under the North Yorkshire Moors. (Massingham says that the Cotswolds are in effect the main torso of the oolite and north of them is a long neck and south of them a 'whiplash of a tail' — like, he says, the outline of the ceteosaurus, one of the dinosaurs which were abundant during the Jurassic period and whose fossils turn up from time to time in the limestone.) Along this whole area the underlying oolite dominates the nature of the landscape and the fabric of traditional buildings. Since it is so attractive as a building stone its use has spread across adjoining areas invading the lias regions as well as the clays. (The upper Thames area between Malmesbury and Oxford, for example.) While oolite buildings are often found well outside their

Left:
Cotswold Hill Quarry, near Ford The real stuff. The stone quarried here on the high Cotswolds behind Broadway is an 'Inferior' oolite known as 'Yellow Guiting' stone – 'guiting' being the local name for the upper valley of the River Windrush. The greater the depth at which it is quarried, the deeper the yellow, but as the stone dries out it turns to a light brownish yellow – 'yellow ochre'. It is to be found in buildings in the Chipping Campden area and in the Oxford colleges. As is clear from the photograph the stone is laid down in what are called 'regular bedding planes' – layers from which extraction in convenient blocks is comparatively easy, if somewhat expensive nowadays. Care has to be taken when building with Cotswold stone to ensure that the most suitable face is exposed to the weather, otherwise it will deteriorate. Although it can withstand building loads it crumbles under intense loading and would not be suitable today as it was in Roman times for building arterial roads.

9

own area, the reverse is not often the case. Apart from the intrusion of cheaper materials like brick, timber and concrete, oolite regions are not themselves invaded by buildings of poorer stone. As Massingham put it, 'If . . . an alien building stone appears along the supposed line of the oolite from southwest to northeast across England, it is you who are at fault, not the house nor the stone underneath. You are off the true limestone without knowing it . . .' And as the Cotswolds are the biggest area of limestone and have the longest building tradition, it is the Cotswold building style that pervades the entire limestone belt.

In section the Cotswolds themselves comprise a plateau of middle Jurassic rocks, mainly oolite, with a steep escarpment overlooking the valley of the Severn and a dip slope falling away gently southeastwards to the valley of the upper Thames around Oxford. The highest point is at Cleeve Hill — 1,083ft (330m) — on the western escarpment and the average height of the plateau is between 500 and 600ft (152-182m). The dip slope of the northern and middle Cotswolds contains a myriad of little brooks with shallow valleys flowing into delightfully named rivers — the Evenlode, the Dikler, the Coln, the Windrush, the Leach, the Churn as they make their way into the Thames. Here the villages and most of the houses are found in the valleys with streams flowing through them. Further south, the River Frome and its numerous tributaries flowing into the Avon, have carved steep-sided valleys hundreds of feet deep, with densely wooded, wet floors. Here most of the villages are found on the hilltops and the farmhouses are set on terraces climbing up the hillsides. The only buildings found along the streamsides are 18th century clothing mills.

Over the millions of years of geological time, the escarpment has been steadily eroded eastwards and this means that in places it has been deeply indented with bay-like recesses called coombes of which the largest is Winchcombe. This erosion has also left behind several outliers — Robin's Wood Hill, Churchdown Hill and the great whale-back of Bredon Hill. Along the convoluted escarpment erosion has also taken away the upper layers of the oolite known as the 'Great Oolite' and revealed near the surface, the lower series known as 'Inferior Oolite' — 'inferior' in this case being a geological reference to its position in the stack, not its quality. Away from the escarpment the underlying rock is Great Oolite — with an average thickness of about 100ft (33m) separated from the Inferior Oolite by a bed of 'Fuller's Earth'. In the south Cotswolds near Bath this Inferior Oolite is only about 30ft thick but in the north round Broadway it is more than 200ft (66m) thick. Over the centuries both varieties have been heavily quarried and throughout the Cotswolds there are numerous quarries, active and disused, where we can get a glimpse into the entrails of the

Left:

River Coln at Bibury 'Here in the garden of the Swan Inn or further on down the village street which skirts the river, you may banish every doubt, if you still nourish any, that Bibury is the fisherman's paradise. You have but to look warily over the low wall to mark the big fish lying with their noses up stream on the watch for any delicate morsel that may come floating down, or the circling eddy which tells you that they are "on the rise".' (Frederick Griggs in 1905.)

The delights of Bibury were not really discovered by outsiders – especially the Cotswold cognoscenti from Oxford – until the end of the last century. From the point of view of the visitor, surprisingly little has changed. The descendants of the trout he mentions have nowadays perhaps developed an appetite for potato crisps and peanuts their ancestors never knew. The spring that rises in what was once the Inn garden 'said to supply at least two million gallons a day' and cooled the Coln so much that it gave the cattle that crossed the ford here a nasty colic, now sustains the local fish farm and puts trout on the tables of the masses. And the Swan Inn continues to be one of the finest hostelries in the Cotswolds – with trout still on the menu, of course.

11

oolite. The best known of these is the disused quarry at Leckhampton Hill on the escarpment just outside Cheltenham. There, apart from that much-photographed 18th century workmen's prank called the 'Devil's Chimney', is a sheer quarry face some 250ft (75m) high that shows clearly the various layers of oolitic 'freestone'. As the quarry lies on the escarpment, the Great Oolite has been eroded and all the rock revealed belongs to the Inferior Oolite series — but not so noticeably 'inferior' in the other sense when built into a glowing city like Cheltenham. The top layers, 20ft (6m) or so, are of ragstone, thin wedges of unevenly-shaped rock usually used for drystone walling and the rougher 'random rubble' walling of lesser buildings. Beneath the ragstone comes the freestone, 100ft (30.5m) of it, starting cream-coloured at the top and progressively turning rusty brown in colour towards the base of the cliff. Variations in colour in the oolite are caused by the presence in the rock of an iron salt called limonite or 'bog iron ore' which puts the yellow into the artist's yellow ochre. The richer the deposit, the deeper the tone. This staining of the lower oolite freestone is particularly apparent in other quarries in the north Cotswolds like the Cotswold Hill quarry near Ford where 'Yellow Guiting' stone is dug. It dries out to a golden brown and can be seen in buildings all round the area and as far east as Oxford. The Great Oolite found in a large area of the mid-Cotswolds is generally silver grey in colour and though workable when first quarried — 'green' as the quarrymen say — becomes very hard once dry. The best known of these stones is Taynton stone which is to be found in the Windrush, Barrington and Taynton areas near Burford and was used in the building of Blenheim Palace. Burford itself supplied stone for the interior of Wren's St Paul's. Similar stone is also found in the Painswick area and was used in the building of Gloucester Cathedral. Further south in the hills above Bath there are numerous quarries producing 'Bath Stone' which is a particularly fine quality Great Oolite which varies in colour from a delicate honey-colour to a rather garish yellow. In the Cherwell valley, north of Oxford, the oolite and the lias immediately below it are heavily stained with iron which imparts to the buildings of the district an 'autumnal tawniness without a touch of grey in it'.

These then are the main building stones of the Cotswold region used for the walls of buildings great and small. The stone-tiled roofs which are such a characteristic of the area — I believe that one sure way of telling when you are entering the Cotswolds is when stone roofs replace slates or thatch — use another stone called 'Stonesfield Slate'. Not truly slates in the geological sense, these 'tilestones' come from a thin layer of sandy limestone at the bottom of the Great Oolite series and have the quality of being split easily, a job usually done by exposing them wet to frost. (Stonesfield tilestones are also rich in 'Thursday-stone' fossils. Reptile teeth are common finds and even rare mammal fossils have been discovered in the past on abandoned quarry sites.) The name comes from a former quarry at Stonesfield near Woodstock in Oxfordshire, but tilestones were also quarried elsewhere in the Cotswolds notably at Naunton, Sevenhampton and in the southeast at Hazelbury, near Box. The Cotswold tilestone industry once employed hundreds of 'slatters' and 'getters' — the 'slatters' made the slates and laid them, the 'getters' dug them out of the ground. Look carefully at the next Cotswold stone roof you see — and notice how the tiles are graded from the little 'cocks' or 'tants' under the ridge stones, through increasing sizes to the 2ft (60cm) wide, 10lb weight 'cussems' at the eaves. Notice too the great skill employed in tiling the valleys between the gables and main roof. Tilestone roofs are immensely heavy and required strong durable timbers like oak, the scarcity of which added increasingly to the cost of such roofs. The industry died out earlier this century when the region suffered from severe economic depression. The only recourse for those wanting tilestone roofs nowadays has until recently been to buy secondhand from demolished buildings. The tilestone itself is still abundant, and there are already signs that in this more affluent age with its demand for authenticity we may yet see a revival of the old craft.

The use of stone tiles for roofing calls for strong rafters and a steep pitch to the roof if the rain isn't to find its way through the gaps between the rather unevenly-faced tilestones. The usual pitch is between 45°-50° but in older buildings, 60° even 65° is not uncommon. This means, of course, that there is a good deal of roof space and whilst this is acceptable in a church, a barn, or even a medieval hall house with its open hearth, it could not be wasted in the ever growing demand for multiple rooms as living standards improved from the Middle Ages onwards. Besides the fitting of dormer windows, a particular Cotswold

Right:
Keble's Clapper Bridge over the Leach, Eastleach John Keble, the Victorian religious reformer and founder of the Oxford Movement, was curate at the twin churches of Eastleach Turville and Eastleach Martin early in the 19th century. Later in life he was active in the great Victorian controversy over creation and evolution inspired by Darwin and others and once declared in hot debate with a celebrated geologist of the day, Dr Buckland, 'When God made the stones, he made the fossils in them'. Keble, who, *inter alia*, had an Oxford college named after him – he died in 1866 – also built this little stone footbridge which still carries his name. It is made from local oolite and God must have put the odd 'Thursday' fossil in it for him too.

solution was to raise the house front in a series of separate subsidiary gables set side by side — often almost touching each other — along the parapet and each with its own ridge the same height as the main roof. Since steep pitched roofs require gable ends as well — hipped roofs are comparatively rare — the prominent gable is the key characteristic of Cotswold architecture either on individual houses or multiplied an hundredfold in villages and towns.

The other main characteristic is the Cotswold window — stone mullions carefully shaped and joined, supporting a stone lintel across several lights, four perhaps on the ground floor, three on the first floor and two in the gable. The casements are of wrought iron and until the end of the 17th century, the glass was lead-mounted in diamond shaped panes. Later, until the end of the 18th century, rectangular panes were more usual. The window is surmounted by a horizontal hood mould called a 'label' which drops at the ends and often turns into a decorated label stop — just as they did earlier around the Gothic windows of churches. Quite often too, where there is a series of windows, the labels are run together in what is called a 'string-course', in effect a drip stone running right round the house. 'Gables, labels, lintels and lights' could perhaps thus sum up the basic Cotswold domestic style.

In the pages that follow, what we have done is to 'follow the oolite', as Massingham would have said, around its main body in the Cotswolds and not only in the physical-geography sense but also in the stylistic sense. The region covered by this book thus goes well beyond what some purists would accept as the *real* Cotswolds — the Cherwell valley, Oxford, even Bath and the valley of the Avon. We have done this to show how pervasive the Cotswold style has been all along the stone belt and had we taken a Massingham's precedent, we could have extended the 'Cotswold Country' from Devon to Lincolnshire but that perhaps is for another book, another day. What we have covered is the 'Greater Cotswolds' — from Banbury to Bath, from Oxford to Cheltenham, Chipping Campden to Chippenham. This then is a portrait of the Cotswold region as seen by one of Europe's greatest photographers of our heritage. What I as editor and author have endeavoured to do is to point out what is of interest and significance in the photographs and, since the Cotswolds have an unrivalled folklore of myths and legends, to look occasionally into some of the stories behind them. For those who would know more of Cotswold stone, Cotswold style or Cotswold history, there is a detailed bibliography at the end.

Alan Hollingsworth
The Hollyhocks,
Broadway

Left:
River Windrush near Burford The Windrush is the largest of the Cotswold rivers flowing 30 miles from its source near Cutsdean to Newbridge in Oxfordshire where it joins the Thames. By the time it reaches Burford it has begun to meander in charming easy coils and it flows through meadows alight, as here, with buttercups and daisies, pollarded willows and hawthorn bushes heavy with May blossom. Across the fields lies Burford itself, dominated by the spire of its church – St John the Baptist that had origins in Norman times and like so many similar churches in the Cotswolds shows in its structure the benefactions of many generations of those who prospered from the wool trade.

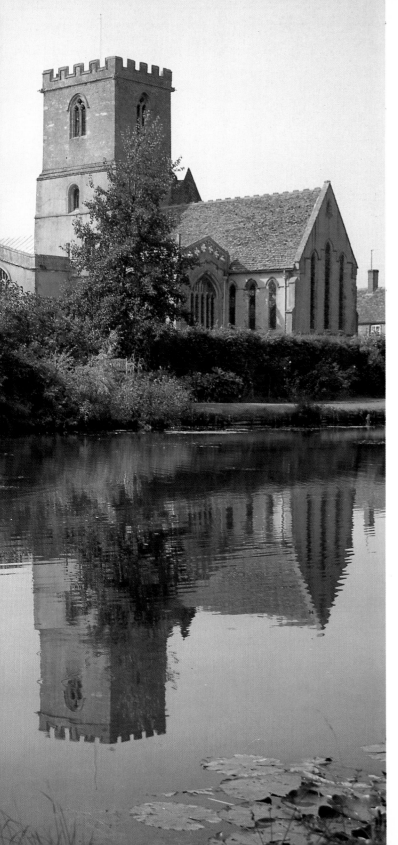

1
Oxfordshire

Left:

Stanton Harcourt Stanton is a word frequently found in the Cotswold area – it is the Saxon word for a 'tun' or homestead in a stony place. In this case the stones are the Devil's Quoits', three large prehistoric stones. The Harcourts were a Norman family and have lived in the manor since 1166. There was a medieval courtyard house on the site until it was largely demolished in 1750 when the family seat was moved to a new house at Nuneham Courtney. Several buildings were left standing, among them a massive detached kitchen block with a conical roof that would do justice to a monastery, the gatehouse now incorporated into the present house and the former northeast tower depicted here to the left of the church. Known as 'Pope's Tower' – one of several – it was probably built c1460. It has the chapel on the ground floor and the priest's lodgings above. The poet Alexander Pope stayed in the rooms in the tower whilst engaged in the task of translating the last volume of *The Iliad* in 1718. The Harcourt family returned to Stanton after World War 2, extended the gatehouse and remodelled the gardens. The house, the tower, the great kitchen and gardens are open to the public on certain days during the summer months. The church, reflected here in a medieval fish-pond, is St Michael's, a Norman church in Cotswold stone remodelled in the 13th century. It contains many ancient tombs of the Harcourt family.

17

Right:

Witney There is a spur of oolite running out to Witney from the west and with its stone-tiled buildings and its centuries of connection with the wool trade, the town is very much part of the Cotswold country. Weaving began here in Roman times first by hand loom and later by using the power of the River Windrush. Witney blankets have been famous for centuries and they are still made in great numbers. One modern factory stands on the site of a weaving mill set up by Thomas Early in 1669 which made blankets for export to the American colonies. In medieval times, Witney was a town of great importance as reflected in the size of its parish church of St Mary with its impressive central tower and tall spire. Originally a Norman church, it was enlarged during the 13th and 14th centuries. The chancel, the tower and the spire with their lancet windows and plate tracery are Early English. Much of the nave was remodelled in the 15th century when the clerestory with its Perpendicular windows was added – all evidence of the continuing prosperity of the wool trade. But Witney's is not a true 'wool church'. This pleasant green with its pollarded lime trees is surrounded by attractive houses of many periods reflecting again the prosperity of the weaving industry.

Right:

Burford High Street As its name implies, there was a 'burgh' – a settlement – on a ford across the River Windrush here in Saxon times. The kings of Mercia and Wessex fought a battle over it in 752AD. The first record of a stone bridge was in 1322. It was a major wool-market until the early 17th century; thereafter it earned its living quarrying stone, making saddles, casting bells, malting, horse-racing, inn-keeping for the coaches, and all the multifarious activities of an ancient market town. Since the beginning of the century it has catered for tourists – university cyclists and walkers from Oxford early in the century, then the motorists who, like the Windrush, began as a trickle and have become a torrent. Burford's variety and its busyness are reflected in the roofline and housefronts of its long steep High Street – gables of every sort, fronts of every period, stone-tiles, dormers and doorcases. It is the same behind the High Street too – a charming mixture of styles and nearly all in the glowing local limestone. It still possesses some of the best hostelries, antiques and book shops in the Cotswolds.

Right:

Taynton The quality of its stone – great oolite with a fine golden tinge to it as can be seen in these charming cottages – made the name of Taynton famous in the Middle Ages. The quarries north of the village had extensive underground workings and yielded several types of stone – forest marble suitable for interior decoration, freestone for the finely jointed masonry we know as 'ashlar', ironstone for troughs and the like, and a white limestone for rough work. St George's Chapel in Windsor was built of Taynton stone; so too were parts of St Paul's and some of the City churches in London. Woodstock and much of Blenheim Palace as well as colleges in Oxford and numerous other lesser buildings also made use of Taynton stone. And with the stone came the masons.

Sir Christopher Wren's leading masons in London in the late 17th century were the Kempsters of Burford and the Strongs of Taynton who were quarry owners as well. In the 17th century and earlier the stone was taken down the Windrush and the Thames in barges and they collected it in carts for Blenheim, but as an Edwardian writer on the Cotswolds put it in 1905, '. . . it is a long and hilly road to the nearest railway station, and the quarries are no longer worked'. Happily they are now being worked again in a small way. It is unusual to find thatched cottages in this area where stone tiles are more usual but tilestones were not produced locally. These cottages would appear however to have been refurbished comparatively recently when tilestones were no longer available. At all events, thatch goes well with Cotswold stone and does not require such massive roof timbers. Pretty gardens are a feature of the Windrush valley.

Overleaf:
Market Place, Faringdon A prevalence of stone buildings and stone-tiled roofs give Faringdon the look of a Cotswold town, but much of the stone is sandstone rather than oolite. It is an ancient town in a strategic position just south of the oldest bridge over the Thames at Radcot and it saw fighting during the Civil War when its church steeple was knocked off by a cannonball. It has been a market town since the reign of King John and at one time called itself 'Chipping Faringdon'. Of interest in the Market Place is the Town Hall standing on Tuscan columns to provide a covered market and dating from the late 17th century. The upper floor was once a magistrates' court but is now the local public library. The Hotel has a Georgian front, but this conceals a medieval courtyard and a delightful Jacobean open staircase which fully justifies the 1645 date over the restaurant door.

Previous page:

Woodstock   The royal manor of Woodstock was used as a hunting lodge for the Woodstock and Wychwood forests from Saxon times until the late 17th century. Ethelred the Unready probably built the first royal manor house, the Black Prince was born there and Henry II kept his mistress — the Fair Rosamund — at Everswell, close to the manor house. He also founded 'New Woodstock' — the present town — to accommodate his retainers. Subsequently Queen Elizabeth was imprisoned there by her sister Mary and the house, by this time a palace, was besieged and badly damaged by the Parliamentarians during the Civil War. Finally the whole demesne was given to John Churchill, first Duke of Marlborough by Queen Anne in 1704 to build Blenheim Palace. In the process Woodstock Manor was totally demolished in 1723. Besides its royal connections Woodstock was also famous for its glove making, a cottage industry which continues today, and for the manufacture of a distinctive type of metal 'jewellery' — sword-hilts, buckles, seals, and the like made using blacksmith's nails in an artistic fashion known as 'Woodstock Steel'. Many of the houses in the town are built of Taynton stone, others in stone from nearby Bladon. Seen here is the attractive Classical style tower of the parish church which was built in 1785. The church itself, of Norman origin, was almost completely rebuilt in 1878. In the foreground is the Bear Hotel, said to date back to 1237, although the present building has a large Georgian block on the left, a lower block in the middle c1700 and an even earlier gabled wing.

Right:

Cornwell   At first glance it looks like the ideal Cotswold village — nestling into the hills, astride a stream, glowing limestone walls, lichened stone-tiled roofs, narrow lanes and cottages comfortably hugger-mugger. In fact it is an estate village and one of the last 'model' villages to be built — or rather rebuilt — and dates from 1930. It was built by Clough Williams-Ellis, the creator of the exotic Portmeirion in North Wales. The village hall is on the left with its bell-tower not in Cotswold but in art-deco style. This is an example of the 18th century idea of the 'picturesque' translated to the 1930s, Cotswold stone but not Cotswold style.

26

Cornishe's Almshouses, Chipping Norton Chipping Norton is the highest market town in Oxfordshire, a reminder that going westwards from Oxford means gradually ascending the Cotswold dipslope. 'Chipping' implies a market and explains the wide High Street. Long associated with the Cotswold wool industry, the town still has a tweed mill. In coaching times it was a stopping place for the London mail on its way to Worcester. In the Middle Ages it prospered with the wool trade and it boasts a wool church built in 1485. These almshouses that have all the attributes of the traditional Cotswold style apart from the prissy little doorheads, carry the inscription 'The work and gift of Henry Cornish, gent, 1640.'

Right:
Great Tew We are on the edge of the oolite here and a long way from the Stonesfield roofing stone, but thatch looks well with yellow marlstone. These cottages probably date from the late 16th, early 17th centuries. Great Tew achieved distinction in the 1630s when Lord Falkland held open house for writers of the day — Cowley, Waller, Ben Jonson, and scholars from Oxford who it is said 'frequently resorted and dwelt with him as in a College situated in a purer air'. It is one of the prettiest villages in Oxfordshire and what was written almost a century ago still holds true today: 'the warm rich tints of the stone have never been seen to better effect than in the cottages of Great Tew. Here it sets off to perfection the tall, many-gabled roofs of thatch, the mullioned windows, the rustic porches festooned with honeysuckle and the trim well-tended flower beds.'

Banbury, Oxon The Fiennes family from nearby Broughton Castle exercised a good deal of influence over Banbury, and some sources suggest that the 'fine lady riding a white horse' that people rode a cockhorse to Banbury Cross to see was in fact a 'Fiennes' lady. At all events, Banbury was not much of a place for ladies with 'rings on their fingers and bells on their toes'. It was renowned for its Puritan bigotry. One old rhyme tells of a 'Puritane' who hanged his cat on Monday for killing a mouse on Sunday. Certainly it was the Puritans of the town who tore down the original cross in Elizabethan times. After the Civil War they blew up the castle. In 1792 they blew up their Norman church with its wool-church Decorated and Perpendicular additions and built instead this Classical temple of local marlstone. The architect was S. P. Cockerell (1753-1827) who built the Indian-style mansion at Sezincote. The style of this church is similar to that of one of Wren's City churches, St Stephen's, Walbrook. The domed tower and the semicircular porch were added in 1818 by the architect's son, C. R. Cockerell (1788-1863). It was a spacious, bright and airy church when built but was ruined like so many more by the Victorian 'improvers'.

Wroxton Another village of glowing 18th century marlstone cottages with thatched roofs and mullioned windows, Wroxton was the site of an Augustinian priory founded in the early 13th century. It was dissolved in 1534 and later became the property of Sir Thomas Pope, a wealthy local landowner who founded Trinity College, Oxford in 1555 and endowed it with the manor of Wroxton with his family as tenants. In 1618 Sir William Pope, his nephew, began building the present house and called it Wroxton Abbey. It was incomplete at his death in 1631 and was not finished until 1858. It has a front of seven gables in the late Tudor style and happily, the Victorians put back the labels, lintels and lights. Wroxton Abbey was the home of Lord North, Prime Minister under George III and the man most responsible for the loss of the American colonies. He is buried in the local church, his tomb surmounted by a remarkable sculpture of Britannia by John Flaxman. Wroxton Abbey is now Wroxton College of the Fairleigh Dickinson University.

2
Warwickshire & Worcestershire

Right:
Bridge over the Stour, near Honington   Like 'Avon', 'Stour' is a popular name for rivers in England — besides Warwickshire, Essex, Wiltshire and Kent all have their 'Stours' and there is even one the other side of the Severn in next-door Worcestershire. The name is said to mean a 'strong powerful river' — but this is one of the smaller Stours and on a quiet day. It rises in the Cotswolds near the Rollrights and flows amiably northwards to join the Avon just south of Stratford, followed by the A34 most of the way. The only town of any size on its course is Shipston-on-Stour where, as its name implies, there was a 'tun' associated with sheep — perhaps a sheepwash at a ford or as a market for Cotswold sheep. It certainly prospered from the wool trade as its legacy of Georgian houses proclaims. This bridge of Cotswold stone with its 22 ball finials would appear to date from 1682 but may well be earlier.

Left and above:

Long Compton and the Rollright Stones As Massingham tells us, the lias thrusts a deep wedge into the limestone in the northwest corner of the Cotswolds giving the geological northern boundary 'the map-appearance of a pair of horns, the broadest and longest cape terminated by Chipping Campden and the much narrower and truncated one to the east of it punctuated by Long Compton and the Rollright Stones'. Although separated by the county boundary, the two are closely linked both geographically and in legend. The facts are that the Rollrights are a Bronze Age monolithic circle that dates back to c2500BC and was used for some obscure religious ritual. They may also have had some astronomical significance but its precise nature is a matter of continuing dispute between experts. Certainly the Druids didn't build them though they may have made use of them to indulge their superstitious fantasies, much as later generations have done. Folk-lore associated the Rollrights with witchcraft, and witches with Long Compton. In the best known legend, a witch meets a king at the head of an invading army and taunts him *. . . if Long Compton thou canst see, King of England shalt thou be*'. A long-barrow of earth gets

in the way and he can't see Long Compton so she turns the King and his knights to stone and there they sit, the King in Warwickshire and the knights in Oxfordshire waiting for the spell to run its course. Meanwhile, Long Compton itself has been sitting quietly under the escarpment enjoying its own witchcraft. As recently as 1875 a labourer there knocked down an old woman of 80 and killed her. His defence was that he was in danger from her witchcraft and had acted in self-defence. That he had drunk a gallon of ale and a bucket of raw cider beforehand was merely to strengthen his nerves. He was found guilty of murder but he didn't hang. He died in a lunatic asylum soon after — from witchcraft, it is said. Long Compton's church of SS Peter & Paul was built in the 13th century and the tower was heightened in the 15th century when it was given its battlements and pinnacles. A clerestory was added to the nave about the same time. The chancel is also 13th century but the whole church was restored in 1862-63. The charming two storied lych-gate arouses a good deal of interest — was it a priest's house perhaps? It is a 16th century cottage with the lower storey removed. The original entrance to the churchyard is down the road.

Right:

High Street, Broadway   The top of Broadway High Street begins the crinkle-crankle climb up Fish Hill, the setting sun glinting on the Cotswolds limestone. Not much inferior about the oolite here — apart from its name. Looking at the smart frontages and cheerful flowery verges and gardens it is hard to realise that at the turn of this century these 16th and 17th century cottages were nearly all derelict and even some of the bigger houses were divided into squalid lodgings. Indeed the whole of Broadway was sadly depressed until the place was discovered by American tourists. As a contemporary writer put it in 1905: '. . . and (it) has continued to be a favourite resort of artists both American and other'. The timber-framed gable is at the end of a row of 16th century cottages with alleys behind them called Shakespeare Cottages. They were condemned in 1930 but rescued and modernised during World War 2 and have been steadily improved ever since. Being a tourist attraction and something of a show village has its compensations. Broadway has in fact attracted travellers since the beginning of the coaching trade in the 17th century when the traffic between Worcester and London had to find fresh horses to get up the escarpment. At one time there were 33 inns and public houses in Broadway. One of them, the Lygon Arms, has an international reputation nowadays.

3
Gloucestershire

Right:
The Coln Valley near Yanworth   The greater part of the Cotswolds lie in Gloucestershire
and running southeastwards from the heights behind the escarpment are the delightful
gentle valleys of the Evenlode, the Windrush, the Coln and the Churn. All have their
particular charm but that of the Coln epitomises all that is best in unspoilt Cotswold
landscape. Rising near Sevenhampton above Cheltenham, crystal clear and alive with
trout, it meanders its lovely, leisurely way through 25 miles of the heart of the Cotswolds
to join the Thames at Lechlade. On its way it passes through water meadows and
wooded hills, through tiny villages and the delightful little towns of Bibury and Fairford.
This photograph was taken near Yanworth not far from Northleach at a point where the
river running between wooded slopes passes the site of the Roman villa at Chedworth. A
prospect that has delighted men's hearts for two thousand years.

Right:

Hidcote Manor Garden, Hidcote Bartrim   The house here is a typical late 17th century Cotswold manor house and was refronted in the 18th century. In 1905, a retired American officer, Major Lawrence Johnston, acquired the property which besides the house then comprised a large cedar of Lebanon, a clump of beech trees and a stream trickling through an escarpment valley that was virtually a wilderness. He terraced the hillside and built walls or planted hedges of unusual plants to form a series of compartments each with its own distinctive colour scheme. Though Cotswold soil is usually inimical to lime-hating plants, pockets of acidity found hereabouts have been bolstered by importing soil enabling rhododendrons, camelias and magnolias to be grown. The result has been a combination of formal planning and informal planting that has been an inspiration to visiting gardeners from all over the world. Major Johnston gave the house and garden to the National Trust in 1948 and the garden (not the house) is open to the public from April to the end of October.

Right:

Stanton This village snuggling into the escarpment was a favourite of Massingham's because of the purity of the Cotswold style of its houses. 'Rounded gables and Renaissance gateways are an intrusion upon the Gothic tradition of the Cotswold style which is as clearly manifested at Stanton as the view of Bredon Hill and the archaic Malverns from its orchards.' As he goes on to point out, some of the cottages here have date labels: 'to show that their looks don't belie them and that they belong to the best period of Cotswold architecture from 1570 to 1650'. The house on the left is Warren House which was the original manor house. It has 'TW1577' engraved over the door of an extension added by Thomas Warren. The cross wing with the prominent chimney breast and the gabled dormer has Tudor windows with arched-headed lights — evidence, as Massingham says, 'that the domestic building of the limestone is directly derived from ecclesiastical Gothic'. The architectural distinction of the village is at least partly due to the careful restoration work carried out by a former owner, architect Sir Philip Stott who bought the estate in 1906. He died in 1937.

Right:

Snowshill Archaeological evidence — Bronze Age barrows and a Stone Age axe — indicates that people have lived here since man first inhabited these islands over 3,000 years ago. Experts in place-names will probably tell you that this 'hill' — 778ft (256m) — on the edge of the escarpment once belonged to a Saxon, or possibly a Dane, called 'Snau'. Locals know better. They point out that the village is on a north face of the escarpment at the head of valley facing north and if there is any snow in the Cotswolds, 'Snozzle' always gets it first. The view here is from the edge of St Barnabas' churchyard. The manor was held by the Abbot of Winchcombe until the Dissolution and the manor house was probably built c1500. At one time it belonged to Catherine Parr, Henry VIII's last wife. The house was bought before the last war by a scholar, artist and craftsman, Charles Wade (d1956) who spent most of his life and much of his fortune accumulating an astonishing collection of artefacts of all kinds from Japanese armour to sedan chairs, from hobbyhorses to ship models. He gave the house and his collection to the National Trust in 1951 and the house and garden are open to the public during the summer months.

Overleaf:

Chipping Campden from the South   Behind
Chipping Campden lies the escarpment
and the Vale of Severn and one prominent
feature is the typical limestone 'mesa' —
flat-topped hill — known as Dover's Hill.
Now owned by the National Trust it is a
natural amphitheatre and Dover's Games
— a sort of Cotswold Olympiad — were
held there every Whitsum Thursday from
c1612 'till the rascally rebellion was begun
by the Presbyterians who gave stop to
their proceedings'. Captain of the Games
was a lawyer born in 1575, Robert Dover,
and a friend of Endymion Porter of nearby
Aston Manor. He superintended events
that included 'playing at cudgels,
wrestling, leaping, pitching the bar,
throwing the iron hammer, handling the
pyke, leaping over the heads of men
kneeling, standing on their hands, etc'.
The 'etc' included the favourite local
pastime of shin-kicking. The Games
resumed after the Restoration in 1660 and
continued until 1851 when they became
such a nuisance in the neighbourhood that
there were again 'given stop' — and by
Act of Parliament. In 1926 Dover's Hill
was threatened by developers and was
purchased by a group of local benefactors
and was given to the National Trust.

In the Cotswolds there are hundreds of
miles of drystone walling like that in the
foreground. Stones laid in this way
without mortar last better than mortared
stone and some of these walls are centuries
old.

Right:

Wyck Rissington   Wyck is the most northerly of three delightful small villages called Rissington in the upper valley of the little River Dikler, 'Little' and 'Great' being the other two. 'Rissington' implies a hillside covered in brushwood and it is of interest that hereabouts clumps of trees are often called not woods but 'bushes'. ('Wyck' probably means that there was a wych elm here, or a dairy farm.) This simple stone farmhouse and cottages clustered around the green give a clear glimpse of what an old Cotswold village — like Broadway, for example — looked like as recently as the end of the last century.

Upper Slaughter   The Eye brook rises in the hills above Upper Slaughter and has cut a deep cleft into the limestone as it flows through both villages before joining the Dikler near Wyck Rissington. They might well be called 'Slaughters on the Water' although there is nothing of Venice about this scene but a great deal, as Massingham puts it, of the 'unique and local genius of the Cotswold style'. 'Slaughter' despite the menace of the name simply means a place with a 'slough' or marshy area, not difficult to find along the brook. There was a local family here who took the name of the village in the 12th century and at the Dissolution took over the local manor and its house that had originally been in church hands. They rebuilt the house — now called the Old Manor — in the traditional Tudor Gothic Cotswold style in the 16th century; it was given a Classical two-storey porch in the 17th century and carefully restored in the 19th century. It is one of the smaller architectural treasures of the Cotswolds. The manor changed hands in the 18th century and as the record of a sale of books there in 1800 reveals, it was then known as 'Slaughter House'.

Right:

Bourton on the Water The water here is the Windrush and despite its modern image as the 'Venice of the Cotswolds' Bourton simply follows the pattern of most of the northern villages in sitting happily astride its stream. Only the Classical style footbridges are different. This one is called 'Paynes' and is dated 1776. Bourton's roots also go deep. Just off the main street are the remains of a pre-Roman camp; there was a Roman settlement here and it was originally a Saxon village with weaving as one of its trades probably as early as the 8th century. One unusual feature is its church. There are very few post-Reformation churches in the Cotswolds — virtually none were built or altered from the middle of the 16th century to the 18th century. St Lawrence was originally a Norman church on a Saxon foundation with a chancel rebuilt in 1438. The church was demolished and rebuilt by William Marshall in 1784 who designed its Classical tower and also kept the chancel. It was rebuilt again by the Victorians who kept the tower and chancel but converted the rest to Gothic. It was carefully done and it is one of the most beautiful Victorian churches in the area.

54

Overleaf:

Winchcombe Seen from the edge of the escarpment not far from the Neolithic longbarrow at Belas Knap, this view shows not just the town but the 'coombe' that intrudes into the western face of the Cotswolds to give the town its name. Langley Hill is on the left with Dumbleton in the distance and on the extreme right is the hillside above Stanway. Winchcombe was a royal seat and capital of the shire of Winchcombeshire in Saxon times when Kenulf, King of Mercia, founded an Abbey here in 798. The town and the Abbey prospered from the wool trade during the Middle Ages and its Abbot had a seat in Parliament. At that time all the land in this area as far north as Snowshill, as far east as Sherborne and as far south as Yanworth were part of the holding of the Abbot. Although some of the farms produced food for the Abbey, most of the upland was a great sheep-run. Around 1320 there were said to have been some 8,000 sheep producing an income of about £350 per annum — perhaps £35,000 in modern terms — and that was only part of the Abbot's income. The prominent church is the parish church of St Peter's.

55

Right:

Sudeley Castle, Winchcombe   The first castle was built here during the troubled reign of Stephen (1135-54) and rebuilt in the mid-15th century by Sir Ralph, later Lord Boteler, who helped to build Winchcombe church. As a Lancastrian he was required to forfeit his estate to the crown when the Yorkist Edward IV came to the throne and accused him of treason although, as he is said to have remarked himself, Sudeley Castle which the King coveted, was the real traitor. The castle remained crown property until 1547 when it was given to Lord Admiral Thomas Seymour who later that year married Catherine Parr, Henry VIII's widow. She died two years later and was buried in the church. Seymour was himself disgraced and executed and the castle became royal again until in 1554 it was given to the Chandos family who held it until the end of the Civil War. It was damaged first in the fighting during that war when it changed hands twice, but more seriously by the Cromwellian 'slighting' that was the fate of many castles during the Protectorate. Derelict and ruinous it was sold to the Dent family in 1837 and they began a process of reconstruction not completed until just before World War 2. Most of the castle itself, as seen here from the southeast, is Victorian although some traces of the Boteler period remain in the shape of the gateway and the Portmare Tower. On the right is the church of St Mary built by Boteler c1460 and vandalised by the Puritans during the Civil War. Desecrated in the process was the tomb of Catherine Parr and her coffin was mislaid until 1782. As part of the restoration of the church and the castle by the Dents, an elaborate marble tomb was designed by Sir George Gilbert Scott in 1859.

Right:

Queen's Hotel, Imperial Square, Cheltenham The biggest hotel in Britain when it was built in 1836-38 by the Jearrad brothers, the Queen's Hotel is a massive example of Greek Revival architecture and its size and design proved a model for the builders of railway hotels all over the country. It is stucco rather than stone and it stands at one end of 'The Promenade', one of the most impressive urban thoroughfares in the country. It has a triple avenue of trees which despite modern traffic still conveys the impression of the country in the centre of town. The Promenade was laid out in 1818 to run from the High Street to the Imperial Spa which later became the site of this hotel. It has an interesting perspective. The carriageway at the upper (Queen's Hotel) end is double that of the lower High Street end which has the effect of making the Promenade seem longer from the Queen's and shorter from the town ends.

Right:

Withington Set in the deeper part of the Coln valley where the hills rise steeply above the village, Withington was the site of a Roman villa destroyed by fire in the 4th century. The village was called 'Withiadun' in the 8th century when it was the site of a nunnery founded by St Aldhem of Malmesbury. Even at that time its abbesses were actively engaged in the wool trade and extended the nunnery's holding of local hill-top sheep-walks. In the Norman era the manor became the property of the Bishop of Worcester: a church and manor house were built and in the usual way, extended and rebuilt in the various Gothic styles over the centuries until the Reformation. The church of St Michael has an elegant Perpendicular west tower, glimpsed here through the trees, and is large by village standards. Richard 'Rural Rides' Cobbett described it as 'like a small cathedral'. The village itself is in two parts on either side of the river. On one side, seen here, rows of old houses gather round the manor house. On the other side of the river another group of houses includes the Mill House and the Mill Inn. Although the Mill House has 14th century origins both it and the Mill Inn were largely rebuilt from old materials in the 1960s, a project that took three years and involved the use of old Cotswold stone which originally came from the demolished prison off the market square at Northleach.

Left and Overleaf:

The Windrush Valley   After rising just south of Snowshill, the Windrush flows southeastwards to Bourton and then southwards to the village that takes its name, its valley widening into broad water meadows, often flooded in winter. The little Sherborne brook rises not far from Northleach and flows eastwards to join the Windrush about a mile from the village. The river then continues eastwards through the Barringtons and into Oxfordshire and on through Burford to reach the Thames at Newbridge. The village of Windrush sits on the hillside above the river, clustered around its church which still has a doorway with one of the finest examples of Norman beakhead work to be found anywhere and as disturbing a selection of leering beasts on the corbel table as the medieval mind could contrive. This is the area of the finest oolite — Taynton stone — and the cottages here and at the next village, Little Barrington, light up like gold in the sunshine.

Right:

Aldsworth This is one of the high bleak Cotswold villages that until the coming of the motor vehicle would have seen few visitors even in summer – except that is for the annual Bibury Races. These were held in the 18th century about a mile or two away off the road to Burford and were attended at one time by the Prince Regent. Aldsworth was also the last place to have the old genuine breed of Cotswold sheep: to preserve it, the Cotswold Sheep Society was founded by Robert Garne of Aldsworth c1892. These sheep – 'Cotswold Lions' as they were called – were large-boned, weighing up to 300lb (136kg), heavy fleeced, with a distinctive forelock covering the face, and were once sold by the thousand at the great market at Stow. Sheared by hand, they produced the wool that made the wool-men rich and built the churches and the manor houses. They are now a rare breed. The church here is remarkable for its spire and the sheer abandon of the enormous carved heads along its corbel table. It also has a powerful peal of bells which, when for generations it had no resident vicar and its parson had to ride over from Turkdean or Fairford, was rung to summon the villagers to church as soon as his gig was sighted from the church tower. The attractive house on the right with mullioned windows is Manor Farm built in the 17th century and enlarged in the 19th.

Right:

Painswick from the Sheepscombe Road Painswick sits high and dry on a spur between two deep damp valleys, its many-gabled oolite houses glinting in the autumn sunshine. (On a more down to earth note, the ploughed field in the foreground also reflects its origins – there is a 'clitter' of limestone fragments and the red tone comes from limonite leaching out of the clay.) Although prosperity from the manufacture of cloth came to Painswick in the late 14th century, as it did to much of the south Cotswolds, it continued much longer than elsewhere – reaching its peak about 1830. The result is that although there are numerous traditional Cotswold style houses in the town, many lie behind Georgian frontages. Genuine 18th century houses are also in abundance and the ambience of the town is Classical rather than Gothic but as Massingham puts it, 'the very Georgianism is subdued to the regional architecture'. Charles I was here twice during the Civil War, the first time in triumphant advance to Gloucester, the second in dejected defeat and the church bears the scars of several encounters. As is evident, it provided a good artillery mark for the Parliamentary gunners and was also damaged when the Royalists smoked out a troop of Roundheads who had taken refuge in the nave, 'firing the doores and casting in hand-grenados'.

Overleaf:

Sheepscombe Its name, one might say, is as old as the hills – it is a Domesday village sitting in a precipitous coombe at the head of the Painswick valley behind the escarpment south of Gloucester. Here the valleys are deeper and steeper than those of the dipslope running eastwards to the Thames. The streams – tributaries of the Frome – are now quite small but at the end of the Ice Age were raging torrents that tore out deep valleys in the soft limestone. Sheepscombe itself heads a valley called the Valley of Peace but not all its history has been peaceful. Following the Dissolution of the Monasteries, there was a spate of enclosure of private and common land sometimes 'by agreement', more often by force and this brought about rioting in the Cotswold area. To put down the protesters, Sir Anthony Kingston, Henry VIII's brutal provost marshal put up a gallows in Sheepscombe in 1549 and made the tithe-collector the hangman, giving him an acre of land for his (and other's) pains. No doubt among these old cottages – some with Tudor Gothic tracery in the windows – is one that was once the Hangman's House.

Previous page:

Landscape at Slad From time to time over the last century or so public interest in the Cotswolds area has been aroused by the nostalgic images portrayed in a best-selling book: Arthur Gibb's *A Cotswold Village*, set in Ablington near Bibury and published at the turn of the century; Flora Thompson's *Larkrise to Candelford* set near Banbury and published during the years of World War 2. The most recent, published in 1959, was Laurie Lee's *Cider with Rosie*, set near here in Slad. The village takes its name from the little Slade stream which runs through a steep and convoluted wooded valley south of Painswick and joins the Frome at Stroud. 'Slad' is in fact another – and rather unattractive word for 'dell'.

Right:

Belvedere Mill, Chalford This is the Frome valley, the course of the old Thames-Severn Canal, and as it winds its way westwards through Brimscombe to Stroud, it is called the 'Golden Valley'. Romantics will tell you that the name comes from the lips of Queen Victoria when she drove through it early in her reign at a time when the hillside beeches were wearing their autumnal gold. Others will point out that the name was first heard in 1777 and almost certainly applies to the wealth created in the valley at that time. As is evident here, both could be true. Chalford was a ford across the river on a drove-road called 'Calf Lane' until the clothing industry developed it in the late 18th century. Belvedere Mill was built at the beginning of the boom period in 1789, the year the first boat travelled from the Severn to the Thames 'amid great rejoicings'. The mill is built of coursed freestone – Great Oolite in this area – but has a Welsh slate roof. The canals made it cheaper to use slate from Wales rather than Cotswold tilestone. The mill produced uniforms for the British Army at the time of the Napoleonic Wars and later for 'John Company's' soldiers in India. There was no room on the wet valley floor for houses and Chalford itself is built on terraces climbing up the steep hillside connected by narrow lanes once used by packhorses and still in many cases, unusable by motor vehicles.

Right:

North Cerney 'Ciren' or 'Cerney' refers to the River Churn that carves its valley right across the middle of the Cotswolds, the border between north and south. North Cerney is also divided by the A435 on its way up the Churn valley to Cheltenham. The church with its saddleback tower is similar in style to that at Duntisbourne Rouse and was originally Norman, rebuilt in the 12th century. The nave and tower were gutted by fire between 1465-70 and were rebuilt at a time when wool money was still plentiful. The battlements and pinnacles on the nave date from this time. The south transept was built as a Lady Chapel c1483. The church has a stone altar originally installed in the 12th century and hidden in the 16th century when stone altars were banned. It was not rediscovered until 1913 when it was re-erected and is still in use. To the right of the church is Old Church House – the former rectory – built c1470 as a hall house with all the attributes of the Cotswold vernacular. Behind it on the hillside is North Cerney Manor, an 18th century farmhouse in local stone with ashlar quoins and a hipped roof.

Right:

Minchinhampton Common A large open plateau surmounts the tongue of land between the Frome valley below Chalford and the deep valley of the Nailsworth stream. Most of it has never been cultivated and has two large commons – Rodborough and Minchinhampton. Bought by the National Trust before World War 2 to control quarrying, Minchinhampton Common has numerous earthworks ranging from Neolithic barrows to modern golf-course bunkers. Most interesting, and just visible here, are the 'Bulwarks', a ditch cut into the solid oolite behind earthworks to protect the common from any approach from the east. They date from the first century AD, the time of the Roman invasion, and one theory suggests that the area was a base established by Caractacus and his warlike Belgic and Silure tribesmen for guerrilla operations against the Roman advance. They run from the Halfway House Inn leftwards across the middleground alongside the Stroud road and are about a mile long. In coaching times this lonely stretch was inevitably the haunt of highwaymen and footpads. Close to the centre of the common where six roads meet is Tom Long's Post which is said to be the spot where highwaymen were buried after appropriate treatment at the hands of the law.

Right:

Tetbury As Massingham puts it, Tetbury sits 'where the thrust of the Cotswold spur parts Thames from Avon (and) is one of those high-standing, wide-spreading little market towns . . .'. Tetbury once had an Abbey – a Cistercian foundation that moved in from Kingswood c1150 and then moved out again. Like most Cotswold market towns, it prospered during the hundreds of years of the wool trade and its architecture reflects those centuries in its changing styles of stone buildings, not always in the Cotswold style but 'the changes step in with an insinuating courtesy to it' – Massingham again. It has also in its time served as a staging post on the coach routes. Evidence of both roles is apparent here. The Market House on the right with its Tuscan pillars dates from 1655 when it served as a wool market. It was altered in 1817 when, presumably, it changed its role to more general marketing. The building on the left is the 'Snooty Fox' which has a ballroom for the Beaufort Hunt on the first floor. Formerly the White Hart, it was rebuilt in the middle of the 19th century in a neo-Jacobean version of the Cotswold style – and in brick cemented to look like stone. Tetbury has a long assocation with hunting – one of its sons was John Wyte-Melville, a Crimean soldier and prolific poet and author of the sporting scene. He was killed in the hunting field in pursuit of the fox which he once described not as 'snooty' but 'mobbed, driven and haunted but game and undaunted'.

Right:

Market Place, Cirencester The Romans built the first city here, the Saxons sacked it in 577 and had built their own 'Royal City' by the 10th century. The Normans came and founded an Abbey here in 1117 and in 1191 the Abbot was made Lord of the Manor. From then until the Dissolution the Abbot dominated the town and its people. 'The Abbot blessed you as rector of the parish church. Your grain had to be ground at his mills on the Churn, and if you were hanged it was upon his gallows and at his orders,' wrote one authority. In 1534 the Abbey was sold on the condition that it was totally demolished. This was done but the church did not belong to the Abbey and was spared. It is, as evident here, a typical Cotswold wool-church and the biggest in the Cotswolds rebuilt in the 15th and 16th centuries. The great porch which dominates the Market Place was added by the Abbey for secular business purposes about 1490. After the Dissolution the townsfolk took it over as their town hall and it was not returned to the church until the 18th century. It was substantially rebuilt in original style in 1831-33 and again during this century. Cirencester itself is built of local stone and has numerous buildings in the Cotswold style – gables and dormers and stone-tiled roofs – but many, as here, have Georgian frontages. One particularly attractive feature is the Park, an estate of 3,000 acres originally belonging to the Abbey but owned by the Bathurst family since 1690. It is open to the public each day.

4
Avon & Wiltshire

Right:
St John's Almshouses, Malmesbury The almshouses depicted were built in 1694 and have incorporated into the wall a Gothic arch from the Hospital of St John which dates from the 12th century. It has a late Norman pattern of decoration of hexagons with inserted lozenges. As is clear from the inscription above it, the new almshouses were built as the result of the benefaction of one Michael Wickes Esq who added £10 a year to an existing annuity 'for Ever' – many hundreds of pounds in today's money. The building itself has some Cotswold style characteristics and has probably lost others in being refurbished over the centuries. It is of local stone, laid as random rubble and now very heavily over-pointed. According to legend, when he built Malmesbury Abbey, St Aldhelm used Great Oolite from Box, opening a quarry for the purpose which still bears his name (Box Ground). The dip slope of the Cotswolds between Bath and Bradford-on-Avon once had many opencast quarries which provided stone for both tiling and walling.

Right:
Church and Manor House, Purton Built about 1600, Purton Manor makes up this charming group with the tythe barn and the parish church close by – a grouping found in villages and hamlets all over the Cotswolds. The church, St Mary's, is of interest because it has two towers. The tower over the crossing has a spire – just visible behind the west tower. The church has Norman origins and is largely 13th and 14th century with a Perpendicular west tower. The manor house is in the traditional Cotswold style and has an interesting doorway which may date from an earlier house on the site. The brick chimneys are a reminder that we are on the edge of the limestone.

Right:

Castle Combe It has been called the most beautiful village in England but Massingham, who would probably have agreed, put it another way: '. . . gabled houses flow down the street like boulders in a mountain stream. The warm, sheltered street looks unreal both for a good and a bad reason. Such beauty as we create in an age of omnipresent ugliness is stark and harsh, and would condemn the village for being ultra-picturesque. Such relativity prevents us from seeing that our ancestors, for whom beauty was their daily bread, built Castle Combe as a matter-of-fact accommodation to the natural conditions of a hill region . . .' The whole idiom of the Cotswold vernacular style is here, gables and labels and hooded bay windows. Interesting too is the absence of verges to the gables – little bonnets reminiscent of Arlington Row in Bibury. Many of the houses were built in the 15th century but have had several face-lifts since then. Further up the wooded valley is the site of the Castle that gives the village its name with only a few earthworks and scraps of masonry left to mark it. It was built c1140 by a Norman family, the Dunstanvilles. The manor house nestling under the escarpment has the By brook running through its grounds and like many Cotswold manor houses has parts dating back to 1360. Castle Combe in common with most of the villages in the Avon valley profited from the cloth industry from the 17th century onwards and the manor house was largely rebuilt in 1664. It is now an hotel.

Left:

Town Bridge, Bradford-on-Avon An important town as early as the 10th century Bradford prospered for centuries from the making of cloth and as its skyline shows, it has an abundance of fine stone buildings in the styles of the successive centuries. Its position shows them off to advantage as its narrow streets climb up the steep north bank of the Avon, rooftop and gable above gable and rooftop. The prominent building with the shaped gables and the angle-turret is the former Town Hall and is the Victorian (1855) version of Jacobean. The bridge itself dates mainly from the 17th century and has nine arches, two of them from the 13th century. The odd building in the middle, set above a cutwater, is the chapel. When journeys were hazardous as they were in the Middle Ages, bridge chapels were much used on departure and return and in the process collected alms from anxious or grateful travellers which helped to maintain the bridge. This one was originally medieval but its cap and finial date from the 17th century when it became a lockup.

Overleaf:

Lacock Village Yet another village that became wealthy from the wool trade between the 14th and 18th centuries, Lacock has been doubly fortunate in that it has been part of the Abbey estate since it was founded and that it continues under the care of the National Trust today. The result is that it has not been prettified to attract the tourists nor has it become a retirement or commuter village. The village is a square of streets filled with houses of various dates and various forms of construction – a reminder that this is the southern edge of the limestone. The street shown here is East Street and on the right is the 14th century Abbey tithe barn; across the road a partly timber-framed house with jettied overhangs and continuing down the street, a lovely collection of gables and labels reminiscent of Castle Combe and Arlington Row with their unverged gables. All are roofed with local stone-tiles and most of the walling came from Corsham. The result is a photographer's dream that Fox Talbot, the inventor of photography who lived in Lacock Abbey, would have envied.

Above:

Tunnel Entrance, Box Isambard Kingdom Brunel's railway between London and Bristol was one of the greatest civil engineering achievements of the Victorian era. Along its length, the most difficult constructional feat was that 'monstrous and extraordinary, most dangerous and impracticable tunnel at Box'. It is nearly two miles long. Three-quarters of it runs through clay, blue marl and Inferior Oolite and had to be lined with brick — 30 million were needed for the task, all carried by horse and cart. The other quarter was the toughest proposition of all — through the Great Oolite — and Brunel planned to cut it in the form of a Gothic arch and leave it unlined. After prodigious efforts by men and horses, the tunnel was completed in June 1841 at a cost of £6.5 million — and the lives of no less than 100 navvies. Despite severe doubts expressed by the eminent geologist Dr Buckland (Keble's Oxford opponent) the Great Oolite section withstood 'the concussion of the atmosphere and the vibration caused by the trains', and parts of it remain unlined to this day. To commemorate what Brunel himself called 'the finest work in England', he designed this triumphal arch over the western exit in exquisite Classical style — and the Great Oolite speaks for itself. As is evident from the plaque in the foreground, after over a century of smoke and steam from countless locomotives, it was restored and cleaned in the 1980s.

Right:
Royal Crescent, Bath Cotswold limestone alight in the sunshine under a lowering sky and in the purest Classical tradition. Royal Crescent was built between 1767 and 1775 by John Wood the Younger on a green hillside above the edge of the city. It has been described as 'the most perfect essay in urban architecture in the western world' and consists of 30 houses with 140 Ionic columns supporting a continuous cornice in the Classical Palladian style. In plan it is a semi-ellipse over 600ft (197m) in length. It was built of oolitic limestone known as Bath stone, most of which came from the quarry at Coombe Down. It was the vision of a Bath entrepreneur, one Ralph Allan who in 1725 realised the potential of the local stone in its suitability for Classical building that led to the development of Georgian Bath and it was he who opened up the quarries at Coombe Down and Hampton Down. Not that everyone is pleased by the Classical glories of Bath. Massingham in his book *Cotswold Country* wryly observes that 'Bath is the only place . . . where the limestone is forced to conform to the Classical style of a particular period. Everywhere else, it is the stone that makes the style, however modified by place and time'. Was he really right?